Space

FaQ

Frequently asked Questions

Written by Valerie Wyatt

Illustrated by Matthew Fernandes

Kids Can Press

For my friend of 40 years, Carroll Maxwell, who coached me through Astronomy at the U of M

Acknowledgments

No book on space could be written without the many excellent resources provided by NASA. Thank you, NASA. My thanks also to the Kids Can Press team who made this book a reality: to Matthew Fernandes for his other-worldly art; to Marie Bartholomew for her out-of-this-world design; and to Liz MacLeod for her stellar editing. I am grateful to Dr. Colin Scarfe, Department of Physics and Astronomy, University of Victoria, for his close reading of the manuscript and many suggestions, and for his friendship. And finally, as always, my thanks to my all-important "first reader," my husband Larry MacDonald.

Kids Can Press acknowledges the financial support of the Ontario Arts Council, the Canada Council for the Arts and the Government of Canada, through the BPIDP, for our publishing activity.

Published in Canada by
Kids Can Press Ltd.
29 Birch Avenue
Toronto, ON M4V 1E2

Published in the U.S. by
Kids Can Press Ltd.
2250 Military Road
Tonawanda, NY 14150

www.kidscanpress.com

Edited by Elizabeth MacLeod
Designed by Marie Bartholomew
Printed in Hong Kong, China, by Wing King Tong Co. Ltd.

The hardcover edition of this book is smyth sewn casebound.
The paperback edition of this book is limp sewn with a drawn-on cover.

CM 02 0 9 8 7 6 5 4 3 2 1
CM PA 02 0 9 8 7 6 5 4 3 2 1

National Library of Canada Cataloguing in Publication Data

Wyatt, Valerie
Space

(Frequently asked questions)
Includes index.

ISBN 1-55074-973-0 (bound)   ISBN 1-55074-975-7 (pbk.)

1. Outer space—Juvenile literature. I. Fernandes, Matthew. II. Title. III. Series.
QB500.22.W92 2002   j520   C2001-901001-X

Kids Can Press is a Corus™ Entertainment company

Contents

Look Up! Way Up!

Some summer night, grab a blanket and take a trip into space. Flop down on the grass, away from city lights and let your eyes roam. With a bit of practice, you can pick out constellations and planets. You might even be lucky enough to see a falling star.

Let your imagination wander farther into space. Float through our galaxy, the Milky Way, then visit other galaxies. Check out a black hole or exploding star — but don't get too close. If you're really brave, let your mind travel all the way to the edge of the universe.

Space is full of questions. Is there only one universe — or are there many? Is there life on other planets? How did the universe begin? Read on for answers to your Frequently Asked Questions about space.

Byte

Want to time travel? Find a star chart (most newspapers have one) and use it to help you locate the Pleiades, a cluster of stars in the constellation Taurus. The light that you are seeing actually left the Pleiades about 500 years ago — around the time Christopher Columbus set out for the New World.

FaQ — Where does space start?

Space starts above a layer of gases called the atmosphere, which surrounds the Earth like a blanket. The atmosphere doesn't stop abruptly; it gradually fizzles out. There isn't enough air to breathe by 16 km (10 mi.) up. Finally, about 200 km (125 mi.) above the Earth's surface, there are hardly any gases left at all. Congratulations — you have just ventured into space!

200 km (125 mi.)

16 km (10 mi.)

FaQ — Is space empty?

No, space is home to streaking comets, hurtling asteroids, blazing stars, swirling galaxies and much, much more. But there's so much distance between things that space feels ... well ... almost empty. In fact, space is *so* big and the distances between objects are *so* great that new measuring units had to be invented. Instead of kilometers and miles, space distances are measured in light-years. One light-year is the distance light travels in one year — 9 461 000 million km (5 880 000 million mi.).

1 light-year | 2 light-years | 3 light-years

Our Place in Space

How fast is Earth moving through space?

Someone should give planet Earth a speeding ticket. It's rotating (turning) on its axis at a speed of 1670 km/h (1040 m.p.h.) at the equator and revolving (circling) around the Sun at an average speed of 107 000 km/h (66 500 m.p.h.).

Our home planet is on the move, yet as you read this book you feel as if you are sitting perfectly still. Why? You only feel movement if you can see things changing position. For example, sit on a stool and spin around. Objects in the background seem to change position, and your brain tells you that you're moving. But here on Earth, even though we're hurtling through space, there's nothing close enough to make us notice the speed.

Why do we have day and night?

We have day and night because Earth rotates on its axis. Turn a ball into a miniature planet Earth and see for yourself.

Mark the ball with an X. Take it outside on a sunny day and hold it so that the X is in the sunlight. If you lived at X, it would be daytime. On the other side of the Earth, which is in shadow, it would be night. Now turn the ball and watch as the X goes from day to night. Earth's rotation gives us our days and nights.

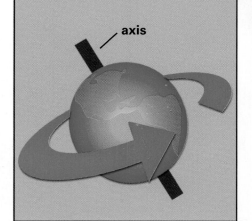

axis

Why do we have seasons?

We have seasons because Earth is on a tilt as it revolves around the Sun. What does tilt have to do with it? Try this with the ball marked with an X and see for yourself.

You'll need

a ball
a black marker
a flashlight

1. Tilt the X toward the light from a flashlight. Notice how much light falls on the X? This is what happens in summer, when the place you live is tilted toward the Sun.

2. Now tilt the X away from the light. See how much less light the X gets? This is what happens in winter, when the place you live is tilted away from the Sun, getting less light — *and* heat.

Here's how Earth's seasons would look from space:

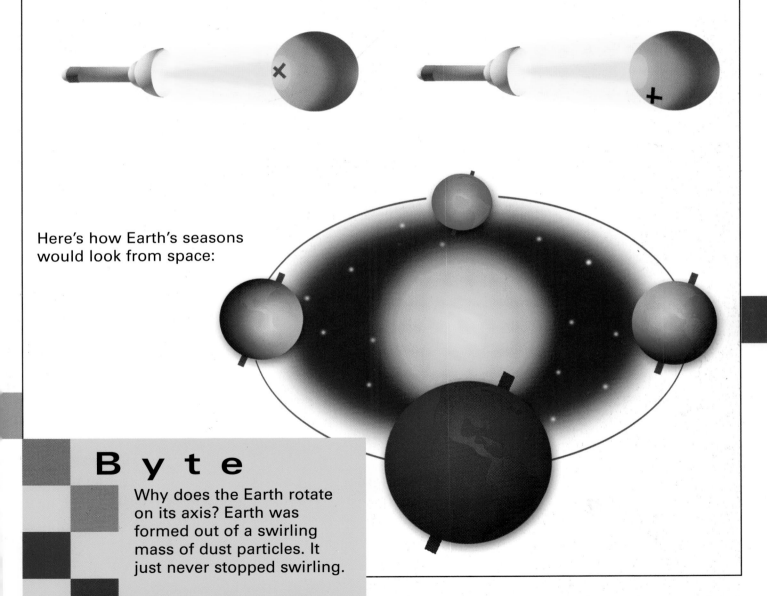

Byte

Why does the Earth rotate on its axis? Earth was formed out of a swirling mass of dust particles. It just never stopped swirling.

Moonstruck

FaQ

How far away is the Moon?

If you could hop on a jet plane and fly to the Moon, you'd want to pack a suitcase because it would take you about 18 days to get there. Although the Moon is our nearest neighbor in space, it's still 384 400 km (238 860 mi.) away.

FaQ

Is it true that we only see one side of the Moon?

Imagine walking in a circle around a friend so that she always sees your face, never the back of your head. In the same way, we only see one side of the Moon.

It wasn't until 1959, when the Soviet spacecraft *Luna* flew behind the Moon and took pictures, that we Earthlings finally saw the Moon's hidden side, sometimes mistakenly called the dark side. (It's not always dark because the Moon rotates, exposing all parts to the Sun's light during the course of a lunar day.)

There were no little green men on the "far side" of the Moon. In fact, that side looks much like the side we see every night.

FaQ

What's the Moon made of?

Moon rocks brought back by astronauts tell us the Moon is made of many of the same kinds of rocks that are found right here on Earth. Just a coincidence? Not likely.

Scientists think that millions of years ago a giant object may have struck the young planet Earth, sending rocky debris hurtling out into space. Eventually, this stuff glommed together and formed our Moon.

Moon rock

Why does the Moon change shape from night to night?

The Moon only *seems* to change shape because different parts of it are lit up by the Sun as the Moon orbits. You can turn a balloon into the Moon and see the Moon's phases for yourself.

You'll need

a light-colored balloon

a standing lamp with the shade removed

a dark room without much furniture

a friend

1. Turn on the lamp and stand as shown.

2. Your friend with the balloon should orbit you in a big circle. But there's a trick: the Moon always has the same side facing Earth, so he should always keep the same side facing you.

3. Turn and watch the balloon as it orbits you. Note how the shape of the Moon-balloon seems to change as different parts of it are lit up. Can you see the phases below?

alien (Moon)

you (Earth)

lamp (Sun)

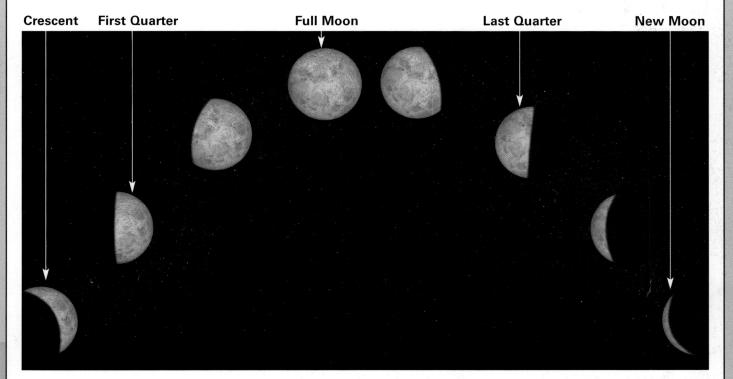

Crescent   First Quarter   Full Moon   Last Quarter   New Moon

FaQ What would it be like to walk on the Moon?

Step onto the Moon and you'd soon have dusty shoes. Dust studded with small chunks of rock covers much of the Moon's surface. This stuff, called regolith, was produced when small meteors pelted the Moon's crust and broke up the surface rock over millions of years.

Take a step and you'd be in for a surprise. Because the Moon's gravity is only one-sixth of the gravity here on Earth, you could take huge, bounding leaps that would make a kangaroo green with envy.

B y t e

The Moon doesn't give off any light of its own. It shines because it reflects the Sun's light.

Scientists calculate that astronauts' footprints on the Moon will be preserved for 100 years or so until the contracting and expanding of the Moon's surface erases them.

The first person to walk on the Moon was *Apollo 11* astronaut Neil Armstrong, on July 20, 1969. The last person was *Apollo 17* astronaut Eugene Cernan, on December 14, 1972. Since then, no one has set foot on the Moon.

The Moon may look small up in the sky, but it's actually 3480 km (2160 mi.) in diameter. That's about one-quarter the size of the Earth.

Is it true that the Moon causes tides on Earth?

It's amazing that something so far away could have an effect on Earth's oceans, but it's true. The Moon's gravity pulls on the Earth. The land doesn't get pulled out of shape because it's solid, but the oceans do. They bulge out on the side closest to the Moon and, to balance this bulge, also on the side farthest away.

The Sun also tugs on Earth's oceans. The bulges — and therefore the tides — are biggest when the Sun and Moon are lined up on the same or opposite sides of the Earth, as shown here.

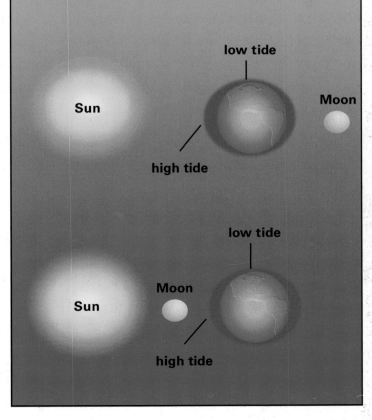

Sun   low tide   Moon   high tide

Sun   Moon   low tide   high tide

Bring on the Sun

FaQ

Why is the Sun so bright and so hot?

The Sun's light and heat come from energy produced deep inside its core. Here, the Sun's hydrogen converts to helium in a process called fusion. This process is similar to what happens inside a hydrogen bomb.

Fusion produces an enormous amount of energy. In a bomb, this sudden burst of energy is an explosion. But, unlike a bomb, the Sun just keeps "exploding" and continuously making new energy. The energy travels up to the surface, where it's released as heat and light.

FaQ

Is the Sun a star?

Yes, the Sun is a star. Like other stars, it's a huge ball of gases (mainly hydrogen and helium) that react to produce energy. The Sun's energy makes life possible here on Earth — it gives us our weather and seasons and provides the light and heat plants need to grow.

But while the Sun is crucial to *us*, by star standards it's no big deal. Compared to other stars, our Sun is middle-sized, middle-aged and a middling producer of energy.

Byte

It takes light from the Sun just over eight minutes to reach the Earth.

Solar flares — huge burps of energy and hot gases erupting from the surface of the Sun — can interfere with radio communications and cause aurora borealis (northern lights) and aurora australis (southern lights) on Earth. (For more on these lights, see page 24.)

Without the Sun, Earth wouldn't have any green plants. The Sun's energy is used by plants to make their own food in a process called photosynthesis. And, without plants, there would be no food for animals and humans.

FaQ

Will the Sun ever burn out?

The Sun has a huge supply of hydrogen from which to make energy. However, one day it *will* use up this supply and go dark.

No need to worry, though. The Sun has been burning brightly for about 4.6 billion years, and scientists think it will shine for another 5 billion or so years. During about the last half billion years, it will become a red giant star. Then it will sputter out and become a white dwarf star. (For more about the life of stars, see page 26.)

FaQ

Is the Sun bigger than the Moon?

They might look about the same size in the sky, but the Sun is actually 27 000 000 times more massive than the Moon. The two only appear the same size because the Sun is much farther away — about 390 times more distant.

In our solar system, the Sun is huge. It contains 99.9 percent of the mass in the solar system, while the planets and their moons account for the remaining 0.1 percent. Stack 100 beans in a pile, then remove 1. The Sun is the pile of 99, and the rest of the solar system is just a fraction of the remaining bean.

Our Super Solar System

What is the solar system?

The solar system is made up of the Sun, nine planets and their moons, plus comets and asteroids. In fact, everything that revolves around the Sun is part of the solar system. This picture shows the nine planets and their orbits around the Sun.

You can see how big (or small) the planets are in relation to one another (they are drawn to scale). But the Sun would actually be much bigger than shown here. If drawn to the same scale as the planets, the Sun would be the size of a plastic wading pool.

Mercury

Venus

Earth

Mars

Jupiter

Saturn

Uranus

Neptune

Pluto

Byte

The farthest-away object found so far in our solar system is a small chunk of ice and rock called 1996 TL66, located 19 billion km (12 billion mi.) away from the Sun. That's more than twice as far as Pluto.

The whole solar system is hurtling through space at about 70 000 km/h (44 000 m.p.h.). Where's it going? It's swirling around the center of the galaxy we live in, the Milky Way.

How did the solar system form?

Scientists think the solar system started out as a cloud of dust and gases. About 4.6 billion years ago, collapsing gases created the Sun. The larger gas planets — Jupiter, Saturn, Uranus and Neptune — formed from the same gases.

Meanwhile, dust particles in the cloud began to stick together. Dust clumps clung to other dust clumps and formed larger balls. Balls collided and stuck together, making still bigger chunks. In this way, the solid planets — Mercury, Venus, Earth and Mars — gradually grew in size.

The Sun was so big that its gravity tugged at the planets like an invisible string, preventing them from flying off into space. Instead, they orbited the Sun. The solar system was born.

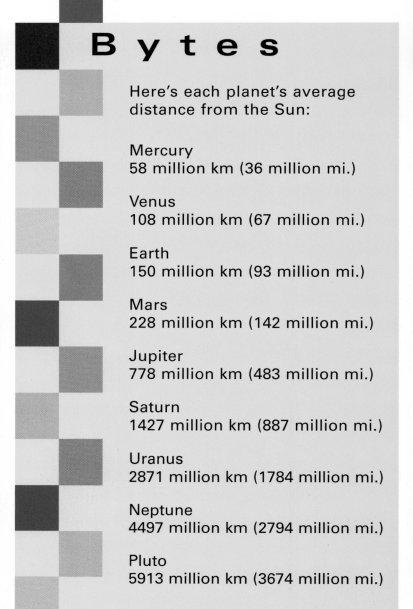

Bytes

Here's each planet's average distance from the Sun:

Mercury
58 million km (36 million mi.)

Venus
108 million km (67 million mi.)

Earth
150 million km (93 million mi.)

Mars
228 million km (142 million mi.)

Jupiter
778 million km (483 million mi.)

Saturn
1427 million km (887 million mi.)

Uranus
2871 million km (1784 million mi.)

Neptune
4497 million km (2794 million mi.)

Pluto
5913 million km (3674 million mi.)

How big is the solar system?

The solar system extends far past Pluto, the most distant planet. But there are only a few million comets, asteroids and small space rocks out there. The planets make up the central part of the solar system. If you could squish all the planets onto this ruler, here's how far apart they would be.

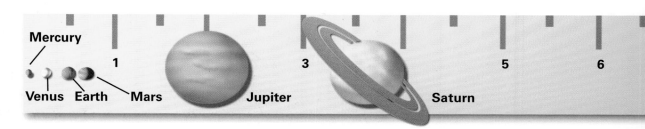

Mercury
Venus Earth Mars
1
Jupiter
3
Saturn
5
6

 **Are there other solar systems?**

There are billions of stars like our Sun, so there are likely to be many with orbiting planets, as in our solar system. Recently, objects about the size of Jupiter have been found orbiting a few nearby stars. These huge objects may be planets in another solar system. However, in space, "nearby" can mean billions of light-years away.

 **What is an orbit?**

Tie a string around a tennis ball and tape it securely. Now swing it around over your head. The path of the ball is its orbit. The ball is held in its orbit around you by the string. In the solar system, the Sun's gravity acts like the string, holding the planets in orbit around it.

All of the planets orbit in the same direction — counterclockwise if looked at from the Sun's north pole. Most orbits are almost circles, although Mercury and Pluto have orbits that are slightly flattened into ellipses.

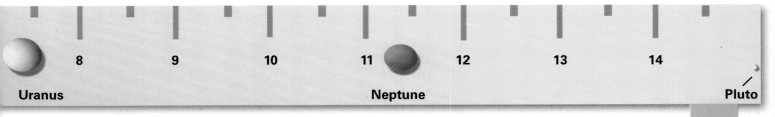

Uranus   8   9   10   11   Neptune   12   13   14   Pluto

Meet the Neighbors

Q&a FAQ

Are the other planets like Earth?

All the planets rotate around an axis and revolve around the Sun the way Earth does. Otherwise, they don't have much in common. Here's how they compare.

Mercury

Description: Small and solid, Mercury's surface looks like the Moon's — pockmarked with craters.

Diameter: 4879 km (3032 mi.), about $\frac{1}{3}$ the diameter of Earth

Length of day: 176 Earth days

Length of year: 88 Earth days

Moons: 0

Claim to fame: The planet closest to the Sun.

Venus

Description: Its thick, poisonous atmosphere holds in heat the way the glass in a greenhouse does, so its surface is always sizzling hot.

Diameter: 12 104 km (7521 mi.), slightly smaller than Earth

Length of day: 117 Earth days

Length of year: 224.7 Earth days

Moons: 0

Claim to fame: The hottest planet in the solar system.

Earth

Description:
Blue and green and wet all over, Earth is the only planet known to have water — and life.

Diameter: 12 756 km (7926 mi.)

Length of day: 24 hours

Length of year: 365.3 days

Moons: 1

Claim to fame: Home to 6 billion Earthlings.

Mars

Description: A cold desert of rusty rock and sand, Mars has high-speed winds that whip its red soil into the air, turning its sky a peach color.

Diameter: 6794 km (4222 mi.), about $1/2$ the diameter of Earth

Length of day: 24 Earth hours, 39 Earth minutes

Length of year: 687 Earth days

Moons: 2

Claim to fame: The planet most like Earth. It may once even have had water.

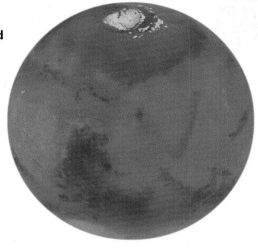

Jupiter

Description: Huge, storm-swept and cloud-covered, Jupiter is made mostly of gases, with a solid core the size of Earth.

Diameter: 142 985 km (88 849 mi.), more than 11 times the diameter of Earth

Length of day: 9 Earth hours, 50 Earth minutes

Length of year: 11.86 Earth years

Moons: 16

Claim to fame: The biggest of all the planets and by far the heaviest.

Saturn

Description: A large gas planet, somewhat like Jupiter, Saturn has rings made of chunks of ice.

Diameter: 120 536 km (74 900 mi.), more than 9 times the diameter of Earth

Length of day: 10 Earth hours, 39 Earth minutes

Length of year: 29.46 Earth years

Moons: 22

Claim to fame: Saturn's beautiful rings are made up of icy particles and chunks of ice-covered rocks. Some particles are as small as peas; the chunks can be bigger than mini-vans.

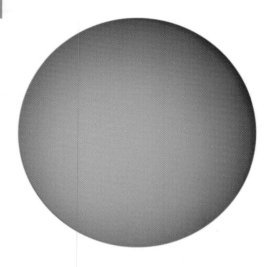

Uranus

Description: With a solid core about the size of Earth, Uranus is mostly slushy ice with a thick blanket of gases.

Diameter: 51 118 km
(31 764 mi.), 4 times the diameter of Earth

Length of day: 17 Earth hours, 18 Earth minutes

Length of year: 84 Earth years

Moons: 21

Claim to fame: Uranus rolls around the sun on its side instead of upright like the other planets. It may have been knocked sideways by colliding with something big.

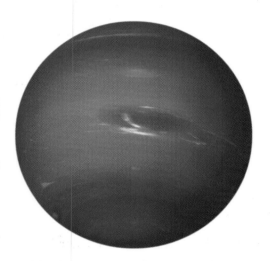

Neptune

Description: So distant that not much is known about it, Neptune appears not to have a solid surface.

Diameter: 49 526 km (30 775 mi.), almost 4 times the diameter of Earth

Length of day: 15 Earth hours, 40 Earth minutes

Length of year: 164.8 Earth years

Moons: 8

Claim to fame: A swirling, windy atmosphere, including a huge, never-ending storm called the Great Dark Spot.

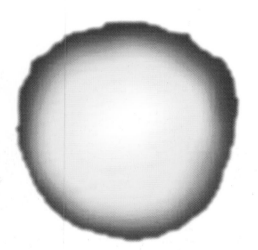

Pluto

Description: Tiny and distant, Pluto is considered a planet by some and an asteroid or a comet by others.

Diameter: approximately 2390 km (1485 mi.), about 1/4 the diameter of Earth

Length of day: 6 Earth days, 9.3 Earth hours

Length of year: 247.7 Earth years

Moons: 1

Claim to fame: The planet farthest away from the Sun, although at times its huge, elliptical orbit takes it inside Neptune's orbit, making it the planet *second* farthest from the Sun. Because it's so far away, there are only faint photos of Pluto.

Byte

While all of the planets *orbit* in the same direction, not all of them *rotate* in the same direction. Uranus, Venus and Pluto rotate clockwise, perhaps knocked into retrograde (backward) rotation by collisions with huge objects.

Having trouble remembering the order of the planets? Try this phrase: **M**y **V**ery **E**ducated **M**onkey **J**ust **S**erved **U**s **N**oodle **P**udding. The first letter of each word matches the first letter of the planets, starting with the planet closest to the Sun (Mercury) and ending with the most distant (Pluto).

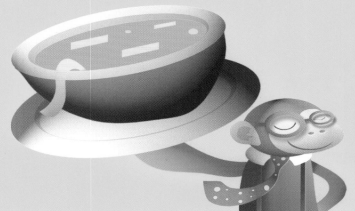

FaQ

Is there life on other planets in our solar system?

Don't expect little green aliens with pink antennae, at least not in our solar system.

Life as we know it requires two main ingredients: moderate temperatures and liquid water. So far, none of the other planets has either, although scientists think two planets may have had these ingredients in the past. Mars has channels in its surface that could be the remains of old riverbeds, lakes and shallow seas, but there's no flowing water there now. Mars is too cold — any water would be frozen solid.

Venus is another candidate. Millions of years ago when our Sun burned less hotly, Venus may have had liquid water. But today its surface temperature is hotter than a pizza oven — too hot for liquid water.

The bodies in the solar system that may have water are two of Jupiter's moons, Europa and Ganymede. But their water, if it exists, is deep under their icy crusts. Is there life in these underground oceans? Only time will tell.

Identified Flying Objects

 **What is a comet?**

Picture a snowball mixed with soot. Now enlarge it thousands of times and send it into orbit around the Sun.

A comet is like an enormous dirty snowball, up to several kilometers (or miles) across, that travels around the Sun on an elliptical orbit. As the comet nears the Sun, its icy surface starts to vaporize (turn into a gas), leaving some of the dust behind in a dirty outer crust. The gas pulls away, taking some of the soot with it. Gas and dust stream out into a tail that can be up to 10 million km (6.2 million mi.) long.

But comets are much more than just snowballs with tails. Some astronomers think they may be the source of life on Earth. Millions of years ago, comets may have bombarded Earth and deposited some carbon-rich soot. This carbon was one of the main ingredients from which the first life-forms developed.

 **What is an asteroid?**

A rock the size of a small boulder — or a large mountain — hurtles through space. Duck! It's an asteroid! Yes, asteroids *have* slammed into Earth. One hit Mexico's Yucatan Peninsula about 65 million years ago, when the dinosaurs roamed the Earth. The impact sent clouds of dust into the atmosphere, blocking the Sun. Plants died and the dinosaurs who ate them starved. So you could say that an asteroid wiped out the dinosaurs.

FaQ

What is a meteor?

A meteor is a blaze of light falling through the sky at speeds of up to 72 km (45 mi.) per second. The light flash is caused when a hunk of rock (a meteoroid) plunges into Earth's atmosphere and vaporizes.

Most meteoroids are completely vaporized on the way down, but some of the bigger ones actually make it to the ground where they are called meteorites. These packages of space material may have traveled from the outer edges of the solar system.

Some meteorites are chunks of asteroids. A few are comets that have used up all their ice and are now just pieces of rock. And one that fell onto the ice at Tagish Lake, British Columbia, in January 2000 may be a sample of the stuff from which planets are made. At 4.5 billion years old, it's the oldest meteorite ever found.

This meteorite, found in Antarctica, is thought to be a chunk of Mars.

FaQ

Could an asteroid hit Earth today?

Small asteroids strike Earth all the time. We call them meteors. But the chances of a huge asteroid smashing into Earth any time in the next 10 000 years are *very* slim. It's even more unlikely that one could sneak up on us sooner than that.

Bytes

The Oort Cloud is a band of comets beyond Pluto. Most comets live there. From time to time, a comet gets jostled out of this cloud and goes into an orbit that brings it much closer to the Sun.

Asteroids are sometimes called planetoids because they are so similar to planets. In fact, one asteroid named Ida even has its own moon!

Asteroids come in a variety of shapes — the biggest are spheres, but there are also slabs, bricks and irregular chunks. Most of them are found in the asteroid belt, a band between Mars and Jupiter that is full of asteroids.

Large meteoroids can break the sound barrier as they fall through Earth's atmosphere, causing a sonic boom or thunder-like rumble.

Strange Sights

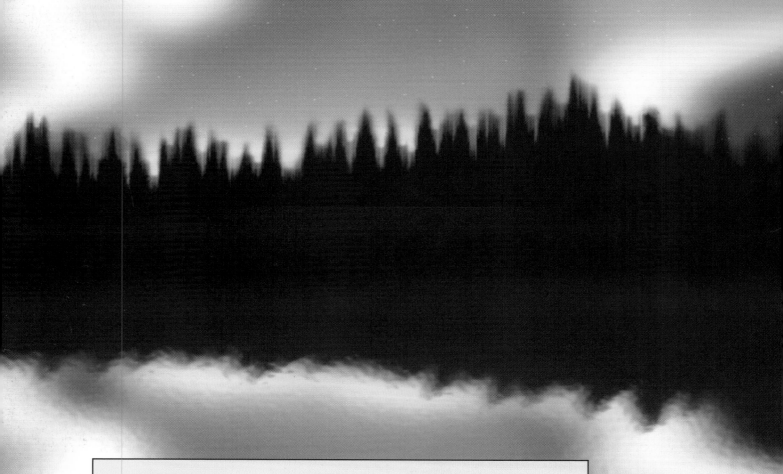

What are the northern lights?

If you look up and see billowing curtains or waving arcs of light in the sky, enjoy the show. You are seeing the northern lights, or aurora borealis. In the southern hemisphere, people see the aurora australis.

These amazing light shows happen when energy-charged particles from the Sun flow into Earth's magnetic field. As the particles hit the gases in Earth's atmosphere, they glow. Earth's magnetic field channels them into patterns that we see as curtains, arcs and other shapes.

 **What is an eclipse?**

Long ago, people thought the Sun or Moon going dark was an omen of disaster to come. Today we know that eclipses happen because of the movement of the Earth and Moon.

Sun — Moon — Earth

Solar eclipse

Sun — Earth — Moon

Lunar eclipse

A solar eclipse happens when the Moon comes between the Sun and Earth, blocking our view of the Sun's light. Because the Moon is smaller than the Sun, it blocks out light for only a small part of the Earth.

If the Earth comes between the Sun and the Moon, it stops the Sun's light from reaching the Moon so it looks dark. (We only see the Moon because it reflects the Sun's light.) This is called a lunar eclipse.

 **What are shooting stars?**

They're not stars — they're meteoroids that burn up as they enter Earth's atmosphere. The burning leaves a trail of light that makes them look like stars shooting or falling from the sky. (For more on meteoroids, see page 23.)

Bytes

A total lunar eclipse can last for 1 hour and 40 minutes, but a total solar eclipse lasts a maximum of 7 1/2 minutes.

Total solar eclipses are very rare, and eclipse watchers often travel great distances to view one.

Stars Above

FaQ Are all stars alike?

From Earth, all stars look pretty much the same. But scientists know there are different sizes and kinds of stars. In fact, stars, like people and animals, go through stages. Here are the stages of a medium-sized star like our Sun. (To see what happens to bigger stars, read about supernovas on page 35.)

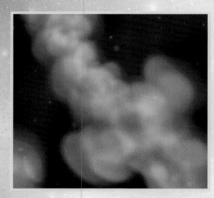

1. Stars are "born" in a cloud of dust and gas called a nebula, as clumps of dust and hydrogen gas are drawn together by gravity.

2. The hydrogen starts to convert to helium, a change that releases energy — just as is happening in our Sun right now.

3. When hydrogen runs low, the star stops producing energy. The core cools and contracts: the outer part expands and glows red. It's now called a red giant.

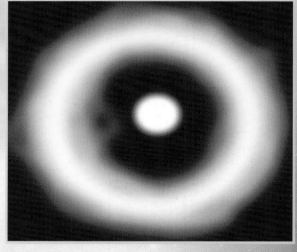

4. With no fuel left, the star collapses and sheds its outer envelope. Inside is a hot ember, called a white dwarf because it shines with a bright white light.

5. Finally, the star no longer glows or twinkles. It's now a black or brown dwarf, the final stage in a star's life.

How long do stars live?

It depends on their size and how brightly they burn. Some massive stars burn brightly and fast. Their lives are short and showy— only a few million years. Some smaller stars burn more slowly and can live much longer — more than 200 billion years.

Bytes

Want to see some baby stars? Look for the Orion Nebula in the constellation Orion (for how to find a constellation, see page 30). The stars in the Orion Nebula are just being born.

The nearest star, after our Sun, is Proxima Centauri. It's 4.2 light-years from the Sun.

At the white dwarf stage, a star becomes compacted and very heavy. A rounded tablespoonful of its matter would weigh as much as an African elephant.

One of the largest stars found so far is Mu Cephei. It's so big that one billion of our Suns would fit inside it.

How are stars different from planets?

Stars make energy in large quantities by converting hydrogen into helium. They produce their own heat and light. Planets don't.

If you're skywatching and want to tell a star from a planet, here's a tip: stars twinkle, planets usually don't. Starlight gets broken up by the movement of the gases in Earth's atmosphere and appears to twinkle. Planets are closer to Earth than stars and appear bigger and brighter. The light coming from them doesn't get broken up the same way starlight does.

Stellar Constellations

Orion

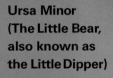

Ursa Minor
(The Little Bear,
also known as
the Little Dipper)

Cassiopeia

What is a constellation?

A constellation is a group of stars. Long ago, people imagined these groupings as people or animals or objects. For example, when they saw this pattern, they imagined a lion.

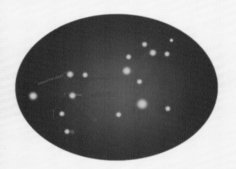

The Lion (also known as Leo)

Seeing constellations helped people find their way around the night skies and that helped them navigate here on Earth. Travelers in the northern hemisphere, for example, used the star Polaris, located at the tip of the handle of Ursa Minor, to tell them which way was north. Polaris (also known as the North Star) doesn't move around the skies as the other stars do, but seems to hover over the North Pole.

In the southern hemisphere, the long part of the Southern Cross points south. Knowing the constellations helped travelers find the stars that would help them navigate.

Lyra (The Lyre)

Pegasus

Ursa Major
(The Great Bear)

Leo (The Lion)

Gemini (The Twins)

Perseus

FaQ

Are the constellations different, depending on where you live?

Yes. The main constellations of the northern hemisphere (north of the equator) are on pages 28 – 29. The main constellations of the southern hemisphere are on pages 30 – 31. Near the equator, you can see both northern and southern constellations.

No matter where you are, the constellations seem to change over the weeks and months. So, for example, the constellations that you see in January won't be visible in June. It's not the constellations that are moving — we are.

As Earth orbits the Sun, we see different sets of constellations. Move in a large circle around a room and keep your head pointed straight ahead. Notice how your view changes? The same thing happens with Earth and the stars that form our sky background.

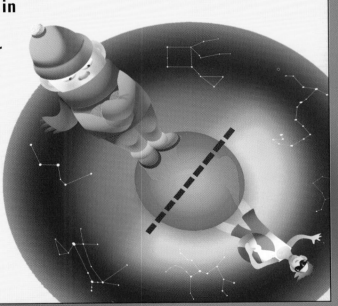

Aquila (The Eagle)

Cygnus (The Swan)

Taurus (The Bull)

These constellations can be seen from the northern hemisphere. Use a star chart to help you find them.

Orion

**Scorpius
(The Scorpion)**

**Canis Major
(The Greater Dog)**

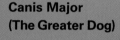 **Crux
(The Cross)**

**Centaurus
(The Centaur)**

**Virgo
(The Virgin)**

 **How can you find constellations
in the night sky?**

You'll need

a flashlight

an elastic band

a piece of red cellophane
bigger than the flashlight
lens

a star guide
(available in most
newspapers)

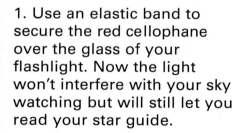

1. Use an elastic band to
secure the red cellophane
over the glass of your
flashlight. Now the light
won't interfere with your sky
watching but will still let you
read your star guide.

2. Take the flashlight and
your star guide out into the
dark and get comfortable.
Use the star guide to help
you find a constellation. Look
for a simple constellation to
start off with — one with just
a few bright stars.

At first, you may have
difficulty finding your way
around. But if you keep trying,
you'll come to recognize the
patterns of the constellations
and be able to move from one
to another. It's a bit like learning
a new neighborhood — only
this neighborhood is light-
years away.

Sagittarius
(The Archer)

Columba
(The Dove)

Eridanus
(The River)

FaQ

Why do some stars look brighter than others?

Some stars are bigger than others, so they look brighter. Our Sun, for example, is only a medium-sized star. There are many stars that are bigger and therefore look brighter — and many that are smaller and seem dimmer.

Other stars only *appear* brighter because they are closer to us. Try looking at a candle up close, then take 30 giant steps away. From a distance, the candle doesn't look as bright, does it? The same thing happens in the sky. Some stars are much closer, and hence look brighter.

And then there are the stars that are bigger *and* closer. Twinkle, twinkle big bright stars.

Corvus
(The Crow)

Bytes

There are 80 constellations in total. At any one time, you can see about 20 to 30.

We see the stars in a constellation as a group, but they may not be anywhere near each other. Some may be billions of miles farther away than others. Here on Earth we can't tell how far away stars are without sophisticated equipment. To us, the stars in a constellation look like neighbors in space.

Grus
(The Crane)

To locate these southern hemisphere constellations, check a star chart.

Carina
(The Keel)

Galaxy Quest

What is a galaxy?

A galaxy is a swirling mass of gases, dust and stars, all glued together by gravity. There are three main galaxy types.

Spiral galaxy

Elliptical galaxy

Irregular galaxy

Spiral galaxies are disc-shaped with a bulging center and several arms. They contain middle-aged stars and clouds of dust and gas where new stars are being born.

Irregular galaxies can be any odd shape. They are the youngest of the galaxies, filled with young stars and lots of gas and dust for making more new stars.

Elliptical galaxies can be shaped like soccer balls or footballs. They contain mostly older stars.

Bytes

The arm of the Milky Way galaxy where we live is called the Orion arm.

Some faraway galaxies emit radio waves or X rays that have been picked up by astronomers. ET phoning home?

Hold on! Our solar system is orbiting the center of the Milky Way at a speed of about 250 km (155 mi.) per second.

555 5555

What kind of galaxy is the Milky Way?

We live in a huge and beautiful spiral galaxy made up of at least 200 billion stars. Our star, the Sun, is located in one of the arms, less than two-thirds of the way from the center. Smack in the middle of the galaxy is an enormous black hole into which nearby stars and gas clouds are falling. (For more about black holes, see page 34.)

• Our Sun and solar system

How many other galaxies are there?

Astronomers have seen millions of galaxies so far. Based on how far apart these galaxies are, astronomers calculate that there are probably a few billion in all. And a galaxy has 10 million to 10 trillion stars.

Galaxies seem to cluster together. The Milky Way galaxy is the biggest and brightest galaxy in a cluster of more than 30 galaxies called the Local Group. It in turn is part of a supercluster called Virgo.

Where can I see a galaxy?

The easiest galaxy to see is our home galaxy, the Milky Way. From Earth, we look out through part of the galaxy, which can be seen as a milky haze on a clear night. To find where to look, consult a sky chart.

If you live in the southern hemisphere, you can also find two nearby galaxies, called the Large and Small Magellanic Clouds. (Magellan was an explorer who navigated by the stars and traveled a long way south.) These two irregular galaxies, located about 75 000 light-years from Earth, are our nearest neighbors in the Local Group.

The Big Picture

What is the universe?

The universe is mostly empty space with a few superclusters of galaxies like dots of light in the blackness. Astronomers believe that the superclusters aren't scattered here and there. They are grouped together. If you've ever blown bubbles in chocolate milk, you've seen how the walls of the bubbles join, with big empty spaces in the bubbles themselves. The universe may be structured in a similar way. The bubbles are the vast empty spaces, while the walls of the bubbles are where you find the superclusters of galaxies.

How big is the universe? It's so huge that it's hard for us to imagine. This might help: if the entire Milky Way galaxy, with all its billions of stars, including our solar system, could be shrunk down to fit on the period at the end of this sentence, the universe would be about the size of a high school gym.

How did the universe form?

About 15 billion years ago, an immense explosion happened called the Big Bang. Our universe and everything in it formed from the gas from this explosion. Scientists think that this is what occurred because the galaxies are still moving away from each other in an ever-expanding universe.

Will the universe keep expanding forever? No one knows, but there are two theories. Yes, say some, the universe will continue to expand until all the stars are dead and there's nothing but a cold and lifeless universe. This theory has been nicknamed the Big Freeze. No, say others, the universe will not keep expanding. Instead, it will eventually collapse on itself, pulled inward by gravity. This theory is nicknamed the Big Crunch.

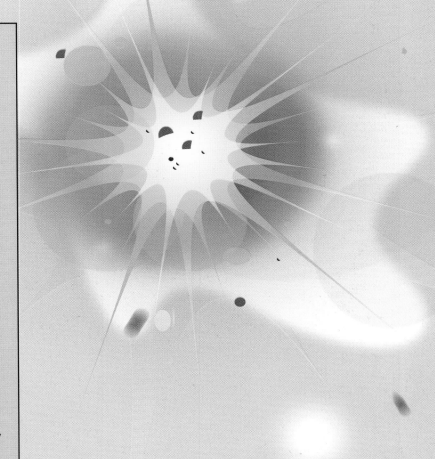

Are there other universes like ours?

It's possible that there are other universes out there. They may be similar — or they may be very different. Think of it. Here you sit on planet Earth in the solar system, which is located in the Milky Way galaxy, which is part of the Local Group cluster of galaxies, which is part of the Virgo supercluster, which is part of the universe, which is part of ...?

Exploring Space

How far can spacecraft go?

Picture this. It's the year 2050. You join an expedition to Proxima Centauri, the star closest to our Sun. Conditions will be rough, you're warned, but you don't care. You'll be one of the first Earthlings to visit the star.

Sound like science fiction? Well it is. In the real world, space travel is dangerous, difficult and slow. Yes, slow. A trip to Proxima Centauri on the fastest spaceship built so far would take about 80 000 years, far too long for any human.

Unmanned spacecraft have traveled farther than manned ones. *Voyager 1*, launched in 1977, holds the record. It's now 12 billion km (7½ billion mi.) from Earth, near the outer edges of our solar system, and will likely keep traveling and sending back data for another 20 years before running out of fuel.

Unless rocket designers come up with a spacecraft that can travel faster than the speed of light, we can't expect to beat *Voyager*'s record by much. And since the speed of light is 299 793 km (186 288 mi.) per second, that seems unlikely.

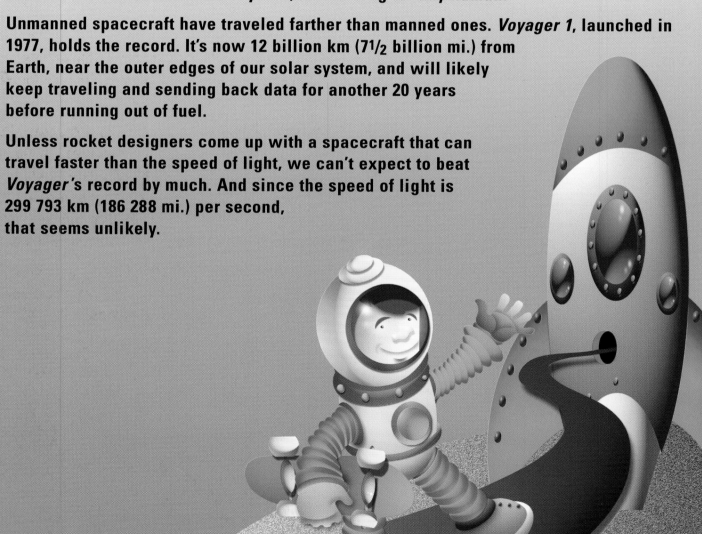

How can we explore farther into the universe?

Telescopes on land and out in space can peer farther into space than we can ever go with spacecraft. In the old days, telescopes let us see the sky more clearly. Today's telescopes look *and* listen. Some do just one job, such as counting galaxies or checking out radio energy. This information provides evidence about faraway objects.

Then astronomers become detectives. They try to decipher what this information means and come up with theories about the universe that fit the data. This is how we have come to know about such things as quasars, black holes and galaxies.

Bytes

Exploring space has its hazards. What if astronauts brought contaminated material back home? Enter NASA's Planetary Protection Officer, a scientist whose job it is to make sure no alien material causes harm here on Earth.

Freeze-dried food, voice-controlled wheelchairs, enriched baby food, firefighters' radios and better school buses are just some of the spin-offs that have come from space exploration.

Why do we want to explore the universe?

We Earthlings benefit from space exploration. By studying the atmosphere of Venus, for example, we may learn more about what the greenhouse effect could do on Earth. By tracking asteroids, we can avoid an impact. Perhaps one day we may even set up a space colony on a moon or planet.

Space exploration also affects our ideas about biology, chemistry and physics. As we see how space bodies behave, we sometimes modify our thinking about these sciences. And that changes the way we see things on Earth.

But most importantly, we Earthlings are curious beings. Now that we can see distant stars and galaxies, we want to know more.

Index